Living THROUGH LOVE

BRIAN ROSCOE

LIVING THROUGH LOVE
COPYRIGHT © 2021 BY BRIAN ROSCOE

All rights reserved. No part of this publication may be reproduced, distributed, or transmitted in any form or by any means, including photocopying, recording, or other electronic or mechanical methods, without the prior written permission of the author, except in the case of brief quotations embodied in critical reviews and certain other noncommercial uses permitted by copyright law.

The content of this book is for general informational purposes only. It is not meant to be used, nor should it be used, to diagnose or treat any medical condition or to replace the services of your physician or other healthcare provider. The advice and strategies contained in the book may not be suitable for all readers.

Neither the author, publisher, nor any of their employees or representatives guarantees the accuracy of information in this book or its usefulness to a particular reader, nor are they responsible for any damage or negative consequence that may result from any treatment, action taken, or inaction by any person reading or following the information in this book.

For permission requests or to contact the author, visit:
brianroscoeauthor.com

ISBN-13: 978-1-957348-01-8

PRINTED IN THE UNITED STATES OF AMERICA

Living THROUGH LOVE

"When you do something noble and beautiful and nobody notices, do not be sad. For the sun every morning is a beautiful spectacle and yet most of the audience still sleeps."
-John Lennon

All the deepest truths in this life are inseparably fused to love. And the only way we can know our truth is to become love itself. That's the journey you have to own. You have to crave it with every thought, celebrate it with every cell in you, and listen as your spirit continuously begs for your alignment with love. This is the path of the spiritual warrior. If you choose, this is your path, and it can light the world.

Our longest and greatest journey is the one where we move our identity, our understanding, and our intuitive nature with one another from our head to our heart. Careful, that destination holds a strength and a sense of self that may prove intense and create a joy that's quite difficult to restrain.

Fresh life may spontaneously erupt through you

Living THROUGH LOVE

Jim Hancock, a long-time friend and patient, came into the clinic one morning. Jim has always been good for an entertaining, often off color but very funny, story of some kind. They usually revolve around his prison days as a county guard. He has a way of humorously discussing things that the average citizen-person would be completely unaware of, making it entertaining and light. But Jim came into the clinic and, with a seriousness, the first thing he told me was that he had made a profound shift in his journey of letting go—letting go of something that has impacted his life for a long time, kind of like releasing himself from his own little thought-generated personal prison.

He said to me, *"Brian, the only way I can think to say it is, the urgency has left me. That frantic sense of urgency around my life, to get things done and to accomplish goals, that push to become a human doing, it's gone. During a workout, I looked at the clock and I had about six minutes left to get some things done, and, suddenly, for no particular reason, the 'lack of urgency' came over me. And I feel free now, finally. It had been with me so long, I think it came from work. In the prison, I had a very demanding superior. I bought into the urgency then, they kind of demanded it and it's been with me ever since, haunting my thinking, and messing with the tension I walked with and my quality of my life. At least until now, that moment in the workout. Finally, I feel free of that feeling of urgency, and it feels wonderful."*

This life is about the healing of the belief systems that we've accumulated from society, family, vocations, and all the factors that have pushed us away from ourselves, our believing that we have to be a particular way, become or believe something that we mistook as important and commonly quite different than our heart-centered truth.

Jim thought his urgency was work-related, that he learned it in his job. This is probably true, however, society pushes us in directions like this all the time. This Western world is built on self-induced urgency, pressure to get things done in line with the opinions of those we deem as important. And when we can walk away from that pressure to perform, walk away from the belief that in order to be successful we need to be a certain productive way… well, who else would we become but ourselves?

If we're stuck in the belief that our life is anything but the creation of healthy love for one another, then we're stuck in some lie generated by this material world, a lie attached to by our own ego. It's often very simply the difference between being stuck in our head or living life through our heart, and there's always a choice to be had.

EXERCISE: List some ways that describe how we/you tend get stuck, the ways that we limit ourselves in our world or live in the ego, holding them tight and preventing our true selves from coming forward. And describe how we let them control our world, maintaining them until we're ready to let them go.

> *"Every time you smile at someone,*
> *it is an action of love,*
> *a gift to that person,*
> *a beautiful thing."*
> *-Mother Teresa*

We are all part of that wild wave fed by the ocean of "what is," filled with life, working, moving through all the shorelines of this world. Building and breaking, waves of love changing everything it touches, moving forward, backward, in constant motion. Does time even exist here? In one million years would we not simply do what the ocean asks of us, trusting its wisdom and reflecting its purpose?

How would you know what your life would be like right now if you had not moved that grain of sand of kindness with a friend, not written that book that refused to go unwritten, not helped that mother with her child in the store, smiled at that quiet soul sitting lonely on the park bench, or somehow blessed that man in need? How would you know what life would be for everyone, had you not decided to more fully live your life, even in small ways? A smile, a pebble of love given, some small courtesy, and an opened and listening heart when you were asked—what would this life be in the absence of all that? It would be less, simply less.

When the deepest intention is one of healing and knowing love, all souls are touched. And though that touch, our touch, may go unseen by many, it's contribution makes a difference to everything and everyone in this world. We hold the purpose of love's abundance in our essence and our heart. Our opinions and our attachment to expected outcomes do not matter, because only the love that we bring forward has meaningful impact on this journey.

Our judgment and ruminations about how life is doing right now, in this moment, is always, at best, an ignorant guess, because movement is always present. We're part of that wave made from the life of the ocean, and it naturally moves forward, we move with it. You're one with this wave of life, your purpose is simple, being the essence energy placed within you, moving the sand on the beach of this world, your sand, your ability to love. Everything we do creates something—its impossible for the wave not to roll, move, scatter the grains of sand, no matter its size. We are made to be part of that wave, of life, of being, and we very naturally move our sand on the beach with each breath. It's our intention that makes the difference in forming this world, and any negativity or fear that gets us stuck in the way of trusting life only wastes our time and limits the quality of what we're creating and our life experience. So live, breathe well, and move sand, create beaches of love. It's in your design.

"It is one of the most beautiful compensations of life, that no man can sincerely try to help another without helping himself."
-Ralph Waldo Emerson

ROSCOE

Thoughts that don't belong in your *heart* shouldn't be given permission to linger in your *head*.

At times, we all struggle with negative, prejudicial, and judgmental thoughts as we walk through life. We might actually feel a bit embarrassed that those thoughts even go through our heads. We say to ourselves, "I'm a good person. How can I think this way?" It helps to stop for a moment and remember where we came from, our history and cultural backgrounds that tend to instill beliefs and stories based in fear into our memory banks and self-image. After we process that, we need to keep our eyes pointed on where we really want to go, pointed toward the truth—our love, our original history.

Living THROUGH LOVE

That painful, judgmental, or prejudicial thought that we so hate to admit is only looking to be healed. We're being given the opportunity to remember that if it doesn't belong in our heart

> The more *grounded* we are in our *love*, the more we can see and respond to our old issues differently. There is a very real *freedom* in that.

JOURNEY PROMPT

Mistakes get made, it's normal. We all do it. We slip, hurt ourselves or someone else—it's part of being human, part of the journey. All the universe requests of you is that you take the time to ask, "What can I learn from this? How can I use this to grow, to become more? How can I use this to help me remember my truth?"

Perhaps this is the reason mistakes get made, why they exist. After all, how can the human spirit spiral upward if it starts out always perfectly centered and performing in pure, unconditional love? How can we grow if we are not given the opportunity to understand what it is to slip into fear? We need to fight for the understanding of our mistakes. We need our imperfections to help us uncover our spirit, to be the catalyst that helps us spiral toward that unknown better within, the prize we were put here to find in the first place.

It may very well be that our movement toward something better is not only crucial for our own growth and touches the journey of those around us, but it resonates into the greater world, and, in some small, incremental way, inspires the evolutionary movement of our entire species. So, by all means, carry on. It's very likely that your work has far more impact in this world than you can imagine.

JOURNEY PROMPT

Work on releasing whatever judgment you can recognize in yourself every day. Judgment comes in many, many flavors. It gets expressed through jealousy as well as sympathy, low self-worth as well as adoration. The list goes on, and none of it is in any way productive to your journey. Rather than indulging it, step back and observe the influence judgment holds on your life. Acknowledge it and set the judgment aside, and look for a better way to see the situation. Then, simply do your best to wish others and yourself well as you move back into your life.

Stuck in the fearful belief that we're all somehow unforgivably different from one another only separates us, alienates us from each other, and and tears us apart.

It's the knowledge that we are all the same that binds us together and helps us see one another with compassion.

When we connect with others in resentful ways or ways that bring up our feelings of ill-will, it helps to step back and give ourselves the opportunity to reboot those emotional responses. It's helpful to our psyche and our own state of wellbeing to find a way to neutralize our negative feelings prior to stepping forward in any way. A good way to do this is by trying to see others as yourself—choosing a gentler, more compassionate lens to view and understand them through.

For example, say to yourself: Just like me, this person can be filled with fear, making choices based in their anguish, and yet, in truth, they only want to know more love. Just like me, this person wants to remember their heart and yearns to see that truth of the spirit radiated into every part of the world through themselves and through all others. Just like me, this person wants to be understood and wants to know what it is to be loved and to love.

Seeing others, no matter who they are, as ourselves is seeing them in their truth, because, in the end, we're all made of the same stuff, the same love, we all come from the same origin. We just want the space to let that unfold.

It helps to remember that our own healing expands outward:

- Healing your heart is not just for you. It expands outward towards everyone.
- Living from your heart is not just for yourself. It expands outward towards everyone.
- Loving one another is not just for you. It expands outward and touches everyone.
- Being kind is not just for you. It expands outward towards everyone.
- Living from your heart is a beautifully selfish thing, just for you, expanding infinitely outward and touching everyone.
- Living from your heart is a beautifully selfish thing to do—an activity made perfectly just for you, so wonderfully explosive, expanding with a passionate touch for all.

Living THROUGH LOVE

JOURNEY PROMPT

Find someone you love to apply this concept of seeing others as yourself to. Find someone you're neutral with, and someone you struggle with, and do the same. Allow yourself to truly see them as yourself and pay attention to your internal response.

NOTE: It often takes repeated efforts to shift yourself into a gentler way of seeing others that you struggle with, but our efforts hold meaning, so carry on!

"Sometimes, reaching out and taking someone's hand is the beginning of a journey. At other times, it is allowing another to take yours."
-Vera Nazarian

No matter who we're looking at, treating people differently from one another because of our fear and misunderstanding only creates attitudes of arrogance and judgment. It plants the seeds of a harsh life grounded in prejudice, distrust, and distraction from our heart.

JOURNEY PROMPT

We all struggle with different judgments or prejudices that hold us back from walking in our love. That's clearly part of the human condition that we all need to address. Can you think of any places where you get stuck, where the lights around you dim as soon as a particular thought or situation, which should be lighter, presents itself? Take note when it comes up. Ask yourself to, at the very least, be open to seeing that situation differently.

Living THROUGH LOVE

Make your life a question for your *heart first*, and then feed the answers back through your mind, *take a breath*, and watch how your thinking and your life changes.

JOURNEY PROMPT

Open your mind to all the questions and answers of the heart. If we were to gratefully embrace all the world's cultures, religions, races, genders and gender identities, weave together all the fabrics of humanity and just love them, just like we love the people and most cherished friends closest to us, to see others with the unconditional love we give a child, how would this world look? Who would we all be as a species? How would we all act and who would we all become in our attempts to love one another with the complete absence of ill will, the absence of our fear, and with heart-centered equality for all?

Living THROUGH LOVE

If you can provide even a small speck of *light*, some little splintered opening to a closed *heart*, especially your own, then you've been *beautifully successful* in this *life*.

JOURNEY PROMPT

Today, take a moment to touch someone with your smile, to call a friend in need and bring a listening ear. Take a second to remind yourself that you're lovable, to appreciate something in your world that's easy to take for granted. Take time to call your mom, dad, child, grandparents, friend, work buddy, partner, or anyone you can think of, and tell them that you're grateful they're in your life and that their presence adds light, ease, or value to your world. Today, take the time to do something loving because, in the end, it's a reflection of your self-love opening to the world. Begin today with love. Isn't that what we all really want?

If we knew of the untold seeds planted and flowers blossomed that manifest through every movement we participate in life with one another, would we ever stop moving with love in this life?

Living THROUGH LOVE

JOURNEY PROMPT

Consider two things you can do to plant seeds of kindness, strength, or love in your world today.

1)

2)

Do your best to pull this exercise off every day. (Abandon conformity. Plant the seeds of your heart freely and with wild variety!)

You know it's out there. It's standing on a chair, screaming your name, like a wild banshee, setting you up to fall down at its feet so it can whisper in your ear. It's running around you like an impatient three-year-old, begging for its mother's attention! Love. It's out there and it wants you!

And what does this *love* want from you?

Well, it wants everything! Every part of you. It wants all that you are. It wants to be a part of everything that you were made to be—in your strength, in your vulnerability, in your heart and your being, and you know in your gut that it already is you. You already are love, and still, love wants all of you!

JOURNEY PROMPT
Where in your life does love not fit? Just where does healthy, compassionate, strong love not belong?

Living THROUGH LOVE

"Resentments give you an excuse to return to your old ways. This is what got you there in the first place!"
-Dr. Wayne W. Dyer

If you knew, beyond a shadow of a doubt, that you are love and that your entire mission in this world is to live victoriously through that love, how would that change the way you walk forward in this life? Would that force you to create a new paradigm to live through? Would your life become more purposeful, more fulfilling, and could it become truer to what you believe you are?

Victorious love is a deep-seated visceral love. It can only be known through the contrast of failed love—living through the pain, suffering, and all the lessons that come from that, and then releasing into the free fall of allowing love a new and better chance.

Beyond the pain of any kind of failed love is knowledge and a deeper understanding of what it is to be human, conscious, and alive. It's in acknowledging that vulnerable part of ourselves that we open the door to a bigger, more breathtaking love—a spirited love that's already inside us and flowing through us.

Living THROUGH LOVE

JOURNEY PROMPT

When you say the phrase, "Victorious love,"

—What does it look like in your mind's eye?

—What does that feel like in your heart?

—Who do you become in it?

ROSCOE

"The roots of all goodness lie in the soil of appreciation for goodness."
-Dalai Lama

There's always a *lingering essence* in the words we use with one another.

Every thought created toward yourself or another has a lingering effect. The essence of that thought (good or bad) stays with us far longer than we imagine and influences our next moment, hour, day, or, in extreme cases, life. When we're aware of the power behind words (spoken internally or outwardly), we can choose to stop them right where there are if they are toxic. We can refrain with compassion. Or, if they're love-based, we can bask in them.

Either way, our words are made of free will choice.

- We can always start fresh by refusing to be a slave to lingering negative interactions or thoughts that bombard us moment to moment, making a brave and fresh effort to transform them so that love, not hate or suffering, is the lingering effect.

- As far as those loving thoughts and interactions, well, luxuriate in the love. It certainly can't hurt.

Mean words linger, so it's better to leave them alone. Love also lingers, and that's just perfect.

JOURNEY PROMPT

Remember: there's always a lingering essence in the words we use with one another, and it goes both ways, but you can only control yours.

Living THROUGH LOVE

Question the *wisdom of the spirit* until the answers make you smile.

JOURNEY PROMPT

Oh! I get it! Love! The answer is always held in the infinite qualities of love… That's definitely worth smiling and laughing over.

REFRAME

I was talking with a patient about the ability to shift our attitude when we're stuck in a bad head space. I mentioned that my daughter, Lauren, seems to have a natural talent to gently reframe her thinking around troublesome friends and difficult moments. When she's mad or disturbed about someone's behavior, she simply makes the personal choice to see that person in a gentler, forgiving way. She offers them a fresh start in her own mind. (It's almost as though she has direct insight into their innocence.) Lauren is a natural master and my mentor when it comes to choosing to position ourselves to step forward in life more lovingly… Well, except with me. I'm her dad. I drive her nutty.

Whenever we can reset ourselves toward love, it's like having immediate and natural access to our hearts and truth in the moment. We all have the ability to look at any of life's situations differently, to refresh our thinking and start again at any moment. It's only a question of opening to it. That gentler place is always inside of you, waiting for recognition, regardless of what you happen to be stuck in. Like Sydney Banks said, "Peace is only one thought away." Sometimes it's really hard to see it, but it is always there, waiting to be seen, waiting to be remembered.

JOURNEY PROMPT

When we're struggling to find our more peaceful way, sometimes we need to step back and say to ourselves, *"I know you're there, wisdom and truth, and I'm having a hard time finding you right now, but you're in me, somewhere, and I will wait for a shift."*

One of the nicest things
ever said to me was,

"I want you to receive the most love that you can from wherever you can receive it."

No restrictions, no concerns—
just wishing me well,
wishing me love, in any of
its truest and infinite forms.

Living THROUGH LOVE

JOURNEY PROMPT

It's great that someone wants for us to receive love, but can we wish that for ourselves? Can we say this to ourselves? "I will receive love from this world wherever and whenever I can." Because it's in our ability to give and receive love that we heal, and, in this, we bring the full presence of what love has to offer to others.

Living in this world is about what and how you love, not about what loves you back. It doesn't require receiving anything from anyone—no rewards for loving are necessary, that's just a redundancy when it comes to giving and being love. If there happens to be a mutuality with love, that's just a bonus—an incredible, beautiful bonus! But like all bonuses, they're just a perk of the job!

JOURNEY PROMPT

Can you think of any times that you've given love with the very real expectation that it "should" be returned in a similar way as it was given? Or has anyone expected the same from you? Can you look back now and see the error in that? What is a better way for us to participate in love?

Living THROUGH LOVE

RECALIBRATING LOVE

*"If truth doesn't set you free,
generosity of spirit will."*
-Katerina Stoykova Klemer

If you're not in this world to learn how to move toward love, what else are you here for? Can you think of a more precious use of your time here?

Remembering love: As you keep your attention on the journey, it happens slowly and insidiously, but it inevitably happens. We might find ourselves living our lives, thinking we're doing pretty well, and suddenly we're sitting, staring into the distance, and wondering who we really are and who we've become in the craziness of this world. And then, in a moment of lucid thought, we remember the miracle, and regardless of what's going on with our outside world, we see that this life is, indeed, *our* own personal miracle—we belong, we're meant to be here, and we, in our wholeness, are love.

> *I was talking to a patient about how when some of us get into our cars we seem to automatically give ourselves permission to project anger, judgment, and aggression. We free ourselves to participate in road rage.*
>
> *I said that we could just as easily use our free will choice and give ourselves permission to be happy and grateful every time we get in the car instead of insane.*
>
> *For some of us, road rage must just be one of our lessons! For the rest of us, it's*

dealing with them that challenges us. But we're here, in this confusing world, to learn those lessons!

My patient and I ended with the phrase: "I mean, you can't do this work anywhere else. That's what this world was made for. So, quit your whining!" And then we giggled at the curiosity of life.

JOURNEY PROMPT

Think about it: If we don't work out our problems, the problems of the heart that we experience while we're here on this earth, where else are we going to have the opportunity to work them out? This place is perfectly designed to draw us back to love, and whenever we decide to take that class, we're automatically admitted! But, all the homework, it's up to us.

Do what you can to love more, to make this journey gentler. Learn how to live so you can identify and get off life's bad rides more easily, more quickly, and feel less beat up afterward.

As for the good rides, have gratitude for them, and open yourself to more of the good you can offer the world.

Your ultimate *goal* is very clearly to open to more *love*.

JOURNEY PROMPT

"Did I offer peace today? Did I bring a smile to someone's face? Did I say words of healing? Did I let go of my anger and resentment? Did I forgive? Did I love? These are the real questions. I must trust that the little bit of love that I sow now will bear many fruits, here in this world and the life to come."
-Henri Nouwen

"Something amazing happens when we surrender and just love. We melt into another world, a realm of power within us. The world changes when we change. The world softens when we soften. The world loves us when we choose to love the world."
-Marianne Williamson

There is no justification for hate. Period!

When we try to deny that fact or fight against it, attempting to convince ourselves that we do have a good reason to justify hating one another, we only end up generating an energetic and emotional shroud of distortion in our minds, which leaves us disconnected from our truth and feeling nothing but separate and isolated from one another.

The emotional shroud generated through choosing to hate draws upon, but is not limited to, these qualities of thought and behavior:

- Rationalizing anger and aggression
- Pointing blame or unjustly punishing those we fear
- Gossip of any kind, or any form of creating pain for others
- Existing in a world of self-important dogmas and less-than opinions of others
- Any and all acts of vindictiveness
- Never truly being able to wish others well
- Relying on anything that makes you not want to attempt love

Living THROUGH LOVE

JOURNEY PROMPT

There are so many ways we find ourselves making the choice to avoid loving one another—choices based in fear and disrespect, anger and taking things personally. It's not an uncommon thing to do. We must release this mindless approach to life in service of mindfulness and compassion.

Can you think of any ways you've participated in the avoidance of love? Any ways you've participated overtly in hate? How did you or how could you do better than you did? How could you ask for that situation to be more fully healed? And are you in a place yet where you want that?

What does your *heart* look like when it's *smiling* into itself?

Living THROUGH LOVE

JOURNEY PROMPT

Your heart smiles when it's immersed in the full and present awareness of its endowed truth.

Your heart finds comfort in its essential peace, in its love, and in the joy of simply being. When we're here, happiness is natural, and fear has little influence.

Live your life with your heart, flowing up into and through your mind, resonating in all the beautiful feelings that lay beyond words, and swimming in its own ineffable love. What does that look like, feel like, and who do you become when you are present to the beauty of the heart? How do your choices change? What's the quality of your thinking here, in this place? How do you see the world? Who do you become when your heart is your guide?

Our job is to do whatever we can to live our lives from a place that requires no imitation outdoor lighting. *Our job is to use what we already have inside to light ourselves.*

JOURNEY PROMPT

In negotiating our way through life and learning how to live it, we can get wrapped up in all kinds of personal judgments, stories about ourselves and others, and belief systems that we've learned from individuals or through society. All this, when we buy into it, can directly impact the quality of our thinking and influence our life experience. We grab onto these stories and judgments in an attempt to understand our world, and they sprout and grow in our minds out of either our superstition, anxiety, fear, or through truth, personal strength, and love. How we attach to our thinking is up to us.

Our job on this journey, however, is to direct the mind towards a life lived in light and love. This is our work, the work of the journey—to build a life where fear is always overcome by kindness and compassion, where the strength of love is always poised to overwhelm any negative or judgmental thinking. We are asked by the essence of who we are to seek out and live in the truth that we hold in our heart, because that's our original objective, that's what we're all here to remember and live.

Healing life asks us to remember our *love*, and to learn how to make friends with our fear.

As we heal our hearts, we begin to understand that we're also transforming who we are. We're busy shifting, shifting, shifting, shifting away from our fear-based habits of the mind and opening ourselves back to a place where fear is only a passenger, not a driver. If we let it, fear would be an annoying and horrible backseat driver, leaving you confused and never clear on where you're going or why. And yet, fear is one of those feelings that makes us human, and although it has its place in times of danger, it usually just needs to be politely ignored, and under no circumstances should it be allowed to take control of the vehicle, you.

Fear can be seen as contrast for the light of our lives. When we ask ourselves without attachment or judgment, "Is this fear or love? Is this a darkening or shading of the light that shines through us?" When we see fear for what it is, we see that it's really only a necessary but benign part of our journey, just another human gift that when seen well has great capacity to guide us toward love.

This ancient journey of healing our hearts automatically asks us to participate in life. Like it or not, we're challenged to step into the process of transforming ourselves and our thoughts back towards our truth and our great capacity for love. Love, after all, is the universal solvent for all the interruptions of a quiet mind.

"If you are waiting for anything in order to live and love without holding back, then you suffer. Every moment is the most important moment of your life. No future time is better than now to let down your guard and love."

-David Deida

Love is not a tradable commodity.
It's everyone's essential resource for life.

www.ingramcontent.com/pod-product-compliance
Lightning Source LLC
Chambersburg PA
CBHW021432070526
44577CB00001B/172